'The light shines through this book. Poetry is a kind of breathing space and Rob Cowen has taken to it. Domestic in the best sense of the word – small scale, intimate, known – it is tender in as many senses of that word as there are. I am deeply grateful for it.' Tim Dee, Caught By the River

'Vivid, beating, aching. *The Heeding* feels like both a eulogy and a defiant, wild challenge to go on. I loved it.' Josie George, author of *A Still Life*

'A dazzling collection of words and images . . . a bold and spirited collaboration.' Helen Jukes, author of *A Honeybee Heart Has Five Openings*

'Poignant and exquisite.' Lucy Jones, author of *Losing Eden*

'Writing that finds light in the dark. *The Heeding* offers a vivid take on a year that weighed so heavily and yet taught us so much. Poignant, powerful, pressing.' Cal Flyn, author of *Islands of Abandonment*

'All books are, in some way, about what it is to be human. But it is rare to find a writer that is able to tease apart the threads that make up the fragile fabric of our loves, hopes and despairs with such care and humility. An exceptionally good book for an exceptionally bad time.' Matt Gaw, author of *Under the Stars*

'A raw, dark and tender, visually stunning, emotionally unravelling distillation of the year in which minutes were endless but whole months disappeared. It's all here – the isolation and connection, the reckoning and recalibration, the loss and revelation . . . Take a deep breath.' Dr Amy-Jane Beer, author of *The Flow*

'Luminously hopeful . . . *The Heeding* is an invitation to appreciate the gifts of the moment, to pay attention to the natural world.' Kathryn Aalto, author of *Writing Wild*

'So powerful, and rich and true. Every line in *The Heeding* feels freshly discovered, full of urgency and clarity. This is an exceptionally moving and beautiful book.' Nick Drake, poet and author of *Out of Range*

'Profound and urgent . . . The poems are raw, heartfelt and often incredibly moving . . . [They] do sing of the dark times, but they bring with them much light. Cowen's poetic observations on the luminous beauty of nature and the fragility of our relationship with it are revelatory and joyful . . . This is a book you will want to share with everyone you care about. It is very special indeed, one to cherish.' Yvette Huddleston, *Yorkshire Post*

'Crammed full of honesty and pain, but touchingly funny, relatable, tender and full of hope. An inspired collaboration with artist and author Nick Hayes, who has produced the powerful, linocut-style illustrations . . . *The Heeding* notices, and pays great care and attention to, the changed world we now live in. A book to be cherished.' *BBC Wildlife Magazine*

THE
HEEDING

ROB COWEN

ILLUSTRATED BY NICK HAYES

Elliott&Thompson

For Rosie, Tom and Bea – RC

For Jessica – NH

CONTENTS

Heed

Origin: Middle English *heden*, Old English *hēdan*,
Old Saxon *hōdian*.

Verb:
1. To mind; to regard; to take notice of; to attend to;
to observe.
2. To pay attention, care.
3. To guard, protect.

Noun:
1. Paying particular notice or careful attention to advice
or warning.

Introduction

On my desk as I write this, sit three things: a fossilised fish in a splinter of stone, a musket ball and the relief of an otter print in plaster of Paris, peppered with river sand from the tiny beach on the Teifi where it was cast. The collecting of such bits and pieces is a habit I inherited from my grandfather. I don't have many memories of him, for he died when I was eleven, but those I do have are mostly set in the neat, little lounge of my grandparents' semi-detached in Skipton. In this room was a cabinet filled with shelves of strange wonders. I recall, among other things, bleached-white animal and bird skulls (fox, badger, sparrowhawk, raven), nodules of dark rock with crystals inside, owl pellets, seashells, birds' eggs, feathers, a seahorse, ammonites, Roman coins, clay pipes, flint arrowheads, pine cones, oak galls, a dunnock's nest and a lead Civil War cannonball he'd found on the hill behind the town's castle. Whenever I visited the house, he would let me pick out a couple of these irresistible curiosities. I'd hold each one and he'd explain something about it. A bit of amethyst might set him off talking about geology and the momentous span of Earth time; a skull could spur on some words about evolution and adaptation. But if I chose the deep, soft, woven cup of grasses, stems and moss that was the dunnock's nest, he'd tell how it had once held a cuckoo's egg; how the hatched chick had fooled the parent birds of another species, edging out their eggs so it might live. Of all his miscellanea, that dunnock's nest and its story stuck. It left me confused, complicating my childish notions of right and wrong. 'Was the cuckoo bad?' I asked him once, and I remember his careful reply. 'No, no. The cuckoo's not good or bad,' he told me. 'It's not like that. It's just listening to a voice inside itself telling it what to do to survive.'

After his death we discovered there were absences from those shelves; things collected that had been kept out of sight. In a box at the back of a bedroom cupboard was a cane swagger stick and a regimental cap badge, dulled dark with time. My brother and I were aware he'd been in the Royal Artillery during the Second World War as our mum had repurposed his canvas gas mask pouch and ammo bags as field-study satchels in the sixties, storing in them her own findings: creatures, soil samples, seeds. These had, in time, come down to us. Yet it was made clear that the subject of the war was never to be brought up with my grandad. School project or not. Mum knew little of his experiences other than there'd been some involvement in an operation that had resulted in high casualties. He'd been promoted 'in the field' to lieutenant, but was in Britain towards the end, achingly close to home in Yorkshire, attached to the anti-aircraft gun batteries dotted around Scarborough and up the east coast to Scotland. What Mum did know, though, was the effect war can have even on those who come home. Over time her father developed symptoms of what would likely now be diagnosed as post-traumatic stress disorder, but what was then very much unseen, internalised, endured. Tics emerged: obsessive timekeeping, states of high stress and anxiety. Even as a boy I remember thinking it odd how we had to call the exact minute we were leaving to visit, whereupon he'd be in an agitated state until our arrival half an hour later. Likewise, after getting home, Mum would call as soon as we got through the door, for she knew he'd be worried sick otherwise.

With hindsight, it's impossible not to discern a link between what was hidden and what was displayed. My grandfather's fascination with nature and history predated the war; he was already a schoolmaster with a reputation for assemblies on trees, fungi and animals – a man who reared, and kept for the rest of its life, a tawny owlet he'd found injured by a road. However, he returned from the war altered. It changed who, and how, he was. I read once how the compulsion to collect can be a symptom of PTSD; how we strive for agency over trauma by transforming it into manageable patterns and order. Certainly, after he came home, nature was a refuge as well as a repository for collectibles. My mother's fondest memories of him are from the days when she was little and the two of them would go off for walks together. Between them they watched, listened and recited the names of what they encountered. These moments remain precious to her partly because she witnessed an unwinding in him: her father lit up with the vastness and magic of a simple stretch of hedge bordering a field, of a stoat hunting or starlings massing at evening. These things provided a displacement; the multitudinous otherness of nature absorbing the obsessive focus and anxiousness he otherwise struggled to turn off. It was an indifferent world he could escape into, yet it was one that surely provided some context and meaning too. For he carried its signs, symbols and markers home, ordering them with, and among, relics of human history as if all were small pieces of an endless jigsaw of the universe. And he attended to all their differences and details with a seriousness, sensitivity and love that was catching. It caught my mother just as it would, later, catch me.

Throughout this terrible pandemic, this year of sorrow, stress, suffering and disarray, I've caught myself thinking back on those shelves of wonders often, and with an understanding that wasn't there before. My grandfather may never have found the words to talk about his experiences, but I've come to appreciate that sprawling collection laid out in a front room as a conclusion of sorts. Or the workings towards one, at least. And, more than ever, it seems to resonate with this moment we're living through, alluding to enquiries, reckonings and truths that echo in this time. Gathered together in my memory, those skulls and shells and eggs and arrowheads speak of a strange, complex and complicated world; one that is human, and yet, gloriously, infinitely, greater than human too. They speak of a world old and dying, yet forever young and changing; they speak of nature – including the human, as part of nature – as something at once beautiful and brutal, unstoppable and fragile, wondrous and terrible, glittering and dark.

They speak of the importance and the power of looking, listening and noticing what's around us, not only for our own solace, but because by heeding what remains in this world we might also learn to listen to the voice inside us, telling us what to do to survive.

◎

This book is born out of a different time and trauma, but perhaps it might likewise be thought of as a collection of things, of findings and workings out – if not conclusions – around our relationships with nature, ourselves and each other at another moment of profound change. Separate pieces that when gathered and arranged together also speak of a need to heed what remains, and what is important, at a point of upheaval and crisis. If you're reading this, you already know the context. Either you have lived through this pandemic or you'll have been taught about it, but you'll know how quickly and utterly the rhythms and patterns by which we lived were altered; how we found ourselves entangled in a struggle for our survival. You'll know how rapidly lockdown, quarantine, isolation, shielding and distancing became new global realities as coronavirus swept through country after country, destroying lives and livelihoods, shocking systems, shutting down economies, driving us inside and sealing us in.

These thirty-five poems follow the arc of an unprecedented year in the grip of this pandemic, from spring to spring; from one (false) dawn to another – one that we hope may prove true and mark the beginning of human emergence and life again. They are a record of, and response to, living through the untethered and uncertain space between. Shapeless, structureless months of absence, grief, desperation, depression, of longing, loss and loneliness, but times during which we've felt the depth and rawness of unselfconscious love and witnessed unexpected moments of kindness, joy and revelation too. They are about what is observed when we're fixed in one place, when our wide horizons become narrowed and confined and our lens shifts to the micro and the close at hand; when all we are is magnified and intensified. They are about coming to terms with the shadow of mortality looming over everything, and what that dark mirror reflects back when we look into it. Most of all they are about the porousness of the borders between human and nature; of how powerfully we affect our world, and it affects us. And how we reconcile and negotiate with something that gives us life and takes that life away.

Reckoning with the blurry edges where humanity, the natural world, history, memory, place, identity and politics meet is an inescapable part of being alive at a moment of climate emergency and the sixth mass extinction of life on earth; at a time when injustice, inequality, discrimination and dispossession remain rife and unresolved. But when the virus came it brought these edges even closer to home. It made them even more immediate, evident and urgent. Amid all the flux and instability, we began to notice and pay attention to what is about us, and what we are about, in ways we rarely do. We took heed because, instinctively, that's how we find our coordinates again in such unmoored times; it's the way we make sense of who we are and where we find ourselves. And it's how we shield and protect that which we love.

I began putting these poems down as a way of processing these proximate edges, of working through and coming to terms with what was being revealed over the unreal, unravelling days, weeks and months. Writing is a natural extension of observing; a constructive outcome of heightened attention – somewhere to put that concentration and imagination, that wondering. Most of these poems began as verse written quickly and open-heartedly; thoughts and emotions that emerged between the strained and constrained hours of work, worry and homeschooling or during nights when I couldn't sleep. Some stayed close to their first draft; others grew and evolved. What I found was that the acts of taking in the details of reality and creating were symbiotic: the heeding resolved into the writing; the writing required the heeding. As I went, the purpose of writing, of creating anything, never appeared so clear: to reach out and give each other the world. To console. To get us through. Indeed, to write is an act of hope in itself, isn't it? The presumption is that there will be somebody to read it. Getting these verses down also became a means of staying true to a vow I made to myself early on in the pandemic: to try to bear witness to the lived experience of unfolding events; as a way of finding the beauty in the destruction and searching for truths. I thought of those Brecht lines: 'In the dark times / Will there be singing? / There will be singing / Of the dark times'. Writing poems felt like a singing of sorts and filled a gap where other attempts at recording what was happening faltered and failed. Why that is I couldn't tell you exactly, but poetry does seem to possess its own magic; a simplicity yet complexity that entangles the reader with its words. It is close, yet reaching, and somehow collective and open to the elements in a way prose sometimes isn't.

One of the first people I shared the poems with was illustrator, and author, Nick Hayes. We've written about similar things before: concerns about our human-centred view of 'nature' and accessibility to land and landscape; the role privilege and power has played in reinforcing the destructive borders between us and the natural world that we so depend on. Nick's idea was to create a book in which the poems were interwoven with black and white realisations of scenes and themes in a continuous visual narrative, connecting and illuminating the verse. Snapshots that similarly spoke of attention and observing and that together would form some kind of meditation on, and a memorial to, this unforgettable moment. It was also Nick who said something to me that has helped define the shape and intent of this book. He spoke of a feeling of catharsis while reading the poems aloud to his partner; a sense of healing in the heeding. I liked that – both the truth in that half-rhyme, the healing in the heeding, and the idea of people being together again, reading to one another.

◎

When I think of my grandad and his shelves of collected things, it's not lost on me that the task of going out with my children to find similar wonders would, in many cases, be impossible. The decline in bird and insect species around farm fields and in the hedgerows near our homes is staggering, and frightening. There are no cuckoos in the woods on the edge of my town. Had the county council had its way last year, there'd be fewer trees too. In their place would have been a new highway. The fact that hasn't happened is down to people. That's worth remembering. We can do things. We have the capability to save ourselves and our environment.

Not since the Second World War has humanity collectively experienced a 'scale' event like the Covid-19 pandemic; an event that has affected so many simultaneously. Just as with that war, our experience has been subjective, but I don't know anyone who isn't in pain or struggling at some level, and I don't believe any of us who have lived through these days will emerge unscathed or without, in some way, being undone. What's important is that none of us emerge unchanged either. Bloodied and wounded we might be, but armed with the hindsight of what we stand to lose, the hope is that we may yet find the strength and will to carry ourselves and our world out of the jaws of catastrophe and destruction. One thing is certain: we'll only get there through being curious and *heeding*; through paying attention, noticing, listening, caring, nurturing, protecting and making the right decisions both personally and politically.

Rob Cowen, March 2021

DUEL

It appears entangled, writhing.
Half-bird, half-beast, hurled from
Heaven, damned and screaming,
quickly descending
over the roof,
into my day-dreaming.

I flinch and duck, and swear,
then turn, as a churning mass
of teeth and feather
sears past my ear and shrieks
over the back wall
into the cobbled street.

An after-image blinked into focus:
chimera. Hawk-wing, talon;
the hiss of a punctured black
bag of biting-back rat,
four legs wheeling,
in empty air.

I open the gate. The world crackles;
the street is electrified by
this earthed thing, locked in
duel with itself, twitching.
A pagan ceremony is beginning:
an old dance of blood and death.

Fur fuzzing, shocked on to walls,
cats in rapt amazement keep distance,
an ache of wildness in their bones,
as a hawk head emerges
and fixes each of us, in turn,
with its manic, yellow eye.

A hooked foot on spine, one on head,
it pins the rat, half-dead yet panting,
to a cobble, a sacrificial table.
Then it bends to rip out a strip
of glistening purple gut
and swallows the lot.

The hissing stops; the buck-toothed
grimace relaxes. Lesson imparted,
the hawk rises, leaving all
the savagery and beauty
of creation imprinted
on this unwitting dimension.

NOISES OFF

Indigo sky pressing down like debt.
All cars quietened; nothing stirs.
Late spring stasis, abandoned, wrecked.
Hell of a thing to be afraid of air.
Of touch. Of family. Of friends. Of work.
To not leave home for four days straight.

Through the wall I hear a hacking cough,
A baby crying, unchecked frustrations,
A barking dog is marking time
For the passing choirs of demented sirens.

I stand in our yard as evening falls,
First time outside all day.
Eyes closed. A blackbird is fluting.
The season's off the hook;
A show no one's attending.
The dog begins again, wound up;
This deathly town, so disconcerting.
Nothing,
Into nothing.
Only darkness noiselessly arriving
Over the long, low exhale of land;
The seethe and tick of insects stirring.

SUNDAY SCHOOL

By ten I was sick of Sunday school.
Raging at the unfairness of an extra chore:
A weekend's hour of bible study
While grown-ups dined on Christ next door.

Colouring cartoon Noahs, Egyptian kings.
Comic-book apostles, the Samaritan, Job.
Envying mates who did more exciting things
Than preparing their soul for almighty God.

This wasn't rebellion; a stance I'd decided to take.
There was no counterpoint (then) to make.
Just an internal flinch at 'Lord of the Dance'
And post-gospel gossip over coffee and cake.

To me, it didn't make much sense
To consign to memory what Jesus did;
To dress in 'best' and parade affluence,
While solemnly praying for starving kids.

And maybe I said something, I don't know.
But on a Sunday jaunt across the moor,
At winter's end, after spring's last snow,
Mum said I didn't have to go anymore.

Then changing tack, splitting scripture to core,
She schooled me urgently and without show.
Priest-like among the curlew, heather and tor,
She told me all I've ever needed to know:

Be kind. Forgive. Attend and heed.
Be strong, but lead with love not power.
Look for the universe inside the seed,
And the face of God in the opening flower.

THIS IS HOW A
SPIDER IS SEEN

A suspension in space blurs focus.
Neither far nor near, throwing out the eye,
Until the cornea adjusts
And the murky mid-distance
Resolves into form and I spy
A garden spider.

This is how it's seen: *between*.
Always between
Uncut new rose stem
And clump of meadowsweet.
Held there, in damp air, on sticky wires.
Backside up, poised

In its silk trapeze.
Such architecture. So fragile.
Especially this morning,
With this ball being volleyed about
And my daughter's clumsy retrieving,
And these sparrows overwatching the yard.

Yet the spider waits in plain view.
Uncowering, unbowed;
Indifferent to chance.
The patience of 300 million years.
Tiger-ish in its livery and penchant
For the merciless god-speed strike.

Uncaring of fate and risk, it sits:
A barnacle-crusted rock, round,
Still. Until, reading what will be
Before it is, eight needle legs
Unfold in a heartbeat to hold on
As the wake of the ball washes over.

LOST

You ask what's happening. I send emails, chasing.
'Will Mummy die? Will I?' Six lost face masks on our
    street;
Splayed, dirty. No one foresaw this defining image of our
    days.
'When can we see our friends?' Soon, I say,
Then buy two old gardening books on eBay,
Knowing it's as pointless as the Rightmove searches for
    houses
We'll never afford. But this is how it is. The longing;
The misjudged commitment to a world already gone.
And it's a small buzz, isn't it? To have things to pin
    hopes on.
Propped up in bed in a room missing a strip of
    wallpaper,
Tired eyes blued by screens, we're searching and
    searching.
A small nightly act of faith that beyond this darkness
There is light: a Promised Land we might step into, keys
    in hand,
Tomorrow. But tomorrow is the same.
'Daddy, what is all that clapping?'
I feel bad about drinking and rush to open windows.

The terraces have emptied. Bewildered by the novelty,
People blink and smile. And you,
Too small to see properly,
Drag the bathroom chair to stand on.
And I overhear you softly cheer,
Make-believing the applause is yours.

'Will you play with me? Mummy's working.' Well, I'm
    working too.
But alright, okay. *'What shall we play?'* But then, what
    timing,
As if it's been watching, and waiting, THAT email drops.
You know the one. *'Daddy?'* Hang on. The close-your-
    eyes,
Breathe-in, swear-under-your-breath kind. I read it again:
'Regrettably, we're cancelling . . .'
And I'm raging anew at this endless unbuilding.
Haven't we had enough? *'Daddy . . . ? DADDY?'* Blink.
    Yes, love?
'What shall we play?'
Why don't you choose? *'Okay . . .'*
*'All the babies are in hospital. Can I have sanitiser and a
    face mask?'*

And quite why it's this question, so innocently asked

And your face turned up to look at me, with its new freckles

And tumbles of curls and Gael eyes, clear as winter skies,

But I think of ageless places, of moor-tops and beacon fires.

And of hushed front rooms at 11:15 with Chamberlain speaking.

And, in a headlong rush, a million mothers and fathers in time,

Lost, like me. Soundless; frightened. Bewildered at suddenly finding

They are staring into a child's eyes, wondering at the storm that's coming.

How they might put themselves between what they love and everything,

And at the scale and weight of the task that is turning

A world on fire into something new, and living.

THE PACT

When you enquired what was growing,
I realised that, without my knowing,
The primrose had flowered.
'The laurel too?'
Yes, the laurel . . . look, I've got to go.
Then when you called the next day,
At the precise minute promised,
I understood what was really happening:
Twenty-four hours of sitting, watching,
Light moving across a kitchen ceiling,
With the oven clock's ceaseless ticking,
Restless hands crossing, uncrossing.
I felt your loneliness like a rush of panic,
As if being told I'd swallowed poison.

It was you who made the suggestion:
A pact to pay attention. Defy this detention,
This boredom, with affirmations
Of life. One word; something observed
Or heard each day. Spoken, texted, whatever,
But filling the space where silence waited.
I sharpened my gaze and gave you:
Goldfinch, chaffinch, starling, sunset.

You answered:
Catkin, blossom, cowslip, sparrow.
And after a month of this I found,
Unconsciously, I was slowing down.
Just as you were finding something new
In each tomorrow.

'Birdsong, birdsong! Did you hear it
At dawn this morning?' Ah, that was mine!
'Fine, we'll share it.' Sunrise, larches,
Earwig, celandine. *'Light, yes!*
The light! You should have seen it,
Shining over the fields this evening.'
We are as children playing a game.
Our pact a key to understanding,
To noticing, as though for the first time,
The interconnectivity of everything.
The way the weave of growing mycelium
Echoes the flow of bird migration.
The way we rush to tell each other, below:
'Swallow! Swallow! Swallow!'

STARLING

We forget that you were once as common as coal,
Little coal-black bird.
Stumpy, dumpy. The wire-dotter, pylon-swarmer.
Camped out on our ledges and trees, screaming
    England's towns down.
Noisy as a classroom on the last day of term.

We forget that you once shimmered through frozen air;
    ripple bird.
Shape-shifter, dusk-dancer. Murmurer, sky-writer,
Endlessly becoming in the darkening gold:
Animals, patterns, waves.
And how we, wonderstruck, witnessed a nightly unity
    against death.

We forget that you stayed true;
Loyal little bird. Roof-flocker, aerial-clinger,
When the rest up and left.
And how you carried the constellations in your feathers,
Iridescent purples, greens and blues, the rare hues of
    petrol on water.

We forget that you were once as common as coal,
Little coal-black bird.
That your blackening of streets and chimney whistles,
Your smoke-like swirling in the skies,
Was an olive branch from heaven.

Yet in the mad pursuit of a spotless life, we believed you
   plague.
We forget that in loss it's the little things that leave the
   largest holes
And that, all along, you were drawing patterns to live by.
Community bird, collaborator, congregator, conversation
   bird.
You, accepter bird, come-together bird.

Crowd bird. YOLO bird.
The dance-like-no-one's-watching bird,
Over town and field, city and sea.
Beauty-beyond-compare bird. Modest bird,
Youth bird. Joy bird.

We forget that you were once as common as coal,
And that fact makes your scarcity more keenly felt.
How losing you is devastating;
A hole both in sky and soul,
For it signifies a greater loss in us.

HONEYMOON

I'd half-forgotten about the half-brick
I hauled back in a bag from Zennor.
But by some confluence this morning,
A sun-line slips through the hanging washing
To spotlight the dark corner
Where it was shoved years ago
In the disarray of moving,
And it's been half-hidden ever since.

I free it. Brushing off a new skin of green,
Remembering its heft in the palm,
Scratching out the curious half-word
Deep-carved across its pockmarked face
In neat font, as if etched by hand.
Three letters,
In a row:
'COW'

In a field falling away towards wintered sea,
The same soft blue of glacial rivers,
We'd walked, wind-deafened, towards a tin-mine
    chimney,
A sky-probing half-stack of blue-grey stone.

Fresh from our vows and seven hours travel, giddy,
Giggling, distracted; drawn to the horizon.
And in my memory, you stumbled over it by that tower,
Half-buried in the grass. Then turned to find what caught
    you.

I peered over your shoulder as you released
Then turned that half-brick rightways up,
Nailing out the dirt. We spoke its word together: 'COW.'
The 'W' abutting the broken edge, suggesting letters
    missing.
'Maybe it said COWEN,' you joked, the same name you'd
    just taken,
'Wouldn't that be strange?' Neither of us really thinking
That fate worked in such obvious ways. That something
So loaded with meaning might appear in that moment, in
    that place.

We'd even laughed that morning, on the journey from
    London,
About your new burden: a life sentence of correcting
The rarity of COWEN spelled not with an 'A' but an 'E'.
How I'd once been drawn down a hospital corridor to
    discover
A relation from his frustrated adjusting of our name's
    pronunciation:
'It's Cow-en, not Cohen,' he was saying.

So the notion that this half-brick might be half-disclosing
Our Gaelic name with its English spelling wasn't worth
    considering.

It was half-right though. And that was enough. So, I took it
    home,
A keepsake from our honeymoon, not yet appreciating
Or fully discerning its significance. Not knowing the half of it.
But imagine the feeling when learning, later, that there was
    indeed
A Victorian maker of firebricks, who hailed from the
    north-east,
But was in high demand everywhere for the ability of his
    wares to
Withstand heat. And that his bricks lined the furnaces of
    mines.

And that his name was Joseph Cowen, with an 'E'.
And in that nineteenth-century mix of nous and vanity,
He'd insisted no brick left his factory without
Bearing his brand: COWEN, our (correctly) spelled
    surname
Stamped on each by hand. And that against all odds,
Burned, broken, that half-brick must have lain for a
    century
On that sweep of Cornish headland, waiting
For us, two halves conjoined, to make its discovery.

You've never been one for omens
Or succumbing to superstition,
Even when the evidence was in front of us, this
    benediction:
A bit of branded firebrick like a founding stone;
Proof we'd withstand the furnace heat of living.
But I've always half-believed it a sign.
And still half-do, instinctively; in the same way that you,
On the phone in the kitchen now, spell our name,
    unknowingly.

THE LOVERS

I dreamed in the night our children were coughing.
Then awoke, to discover it was someone laughing.

I crept through the house to a window at the back,
Where a boy and a girl, nineteen, if that,

Were locked in the street below. Star-crossed lovers,
Hidden from the world, from fathers and mothers,

Who presumably forbade such contact, yet these two
Had defied them in this late-night rendezvous.

Now, reasons for being outside are concrete-set:
A form of exercise? Well, you might argue that.

He was certainly burning calories down there,
Pants round his ankles, backside bare.

Travelling to work? I wouldn't like to say.
Not everybody commutes in the same way.

Is it a medical need? Well, that's harder to claim.
But didn't Michael Douglas once insist the same?

No. Though it's only permitted 'infrequently',
I'd say they were getting their basic necessities.

SOLIDARITY ON A
SATURDAY NIGHT

Hey neighbour, could you do me a favour
and switch on those lights again tonight?
Slung around your backyard's corner,
I thought of lanterns on a masthead; a bright
spot in this lonely dark. So, I switched on ours
and lo and behold:
the house on the other side did the same.
And just like that we formed a chain.
And in some small way, I felt human again.

LAST BREATHS

Alone, in a nursing home, his last breaths begin.
Slow, desperate, shallow at best. He's aware
Of dragging the very dregs from the too-warm air.
Of drowning in this magnolia box. Panicking,
His brain slips like a dog on a wooden floor,
Summoned from sleep by a rap at the door.
Wires, cables, dimmed light; vegetable stink.
Mouth too dry to moan. Too frail to kick or swim.
Gasps are futile attempts to fill lungs already done.
While an alarm in some other corridor sounds.
And no one comes.
Helpless here, he is a relic of another time.
A century or more tree-ringed into his bones.
An unwilling ghost of that *Very* England; of England
    before irony,
Before the sixties. Still soot-black, rough-handed; mire
    and pit.
Where the striving was for respectability. Honour, duty.
What would the neighbours say? All that King and
    Country shit,
A shape in which he would never fit. What with mother
    remarried.
And he, a boy-shaped memorial to a missing man, belted

Nightly for the impertinence of living. Where war,

When it came, was relief. Where he saw,

With those now half-blind, brimming eyes, flies

Crawling out of open mouths.

Where he returned and burned his clothes and went to
    ground

In Gloucestershire. Director of his own fate.

Trimmed in farm coat, wading through ancient clod and
    clay.

Yet he lies now a 5'9 core sample of change;

The human evidence of decay,

Witness to folding empires and summers gathering hay.

He is a prop from an old play, curtained and mothballed

Like the stuffed, lacquered trout, 'Capt. A Lockwood, 6lb.',

He used to admire in the nicotined hall of the Crown.

Aged twenty-nine, waiting to piss,

With post-harvest pint of mild and brown.

He thinks of these things, and of an adored daughter,

Gone at eight: *Margaret. Maggie.*

And another in Rochdale: *Betty,*

Frantic to see him and yet

Kept away for safety's sake. *Stay home. Protect . . .*

And of a wife so loved, outlived. And fishing a river,

At dawn somewhere, 1981; that moment when,
    so aware,
So overcome, that for the first time he knew what it
    was to be alive. And cried.
Now his ravaged body and last, few insufficient breaths
Usher in awareness again: death.
And with each emptying wheeze
He sees his father drawing closer to the bed.
Recognisable from the photograph
Taken on his last leave, the same weekend he was
    conceived.
He moves his hand, and he feels it held and squeezed.
Behind it, a nurse stands raw-eyed in PPE
Saying: *'It's alright. I'm here now. You're with me.'*

MOON OVER
SKIPTON ROAD

'*It's not rising,*' you said,
Voice like a glass-blown note;
Fingers finding mine and gripping,
'*We're turning and tipping to meet it.*'

So young and confident,
So capable of thought.
So entranced and fascinated
By that book we bought.

You were right, of course; we were,
Tipping to meet that expectant face
As it crested terraces with its ghostly light
And silvered a sea of dirty slates.

Then it hung, in stillness, blackness,
Right there, for a moment, alone.
As though arranged entirely for us;
A perfect disc of polished bone.

And before the clouds hurried to hide it,
Like a secret, there was just us three;
The moon, you and me.
And in that second, I remember thinking:

Should these measures prove useless
And I be torn from you,
If it turns out my life
Held no other purpose

But to hold your hand
For this second or two,
It was still worth living for, my love.
You were still worth living for.

MOTORWAY HAWK

There you are, again. A fly on the windscreen
becoming hawk hovering over hedge.
Fluttering, trembling. Always at the edge
of vision. Grey, head-locked; a mottled dot
tacked to the uneven, dirty-linen wall of sky
ahead of a pair of frantic flickering wings.
Like a butterfly alive yet already pinned.
I saw you first from a backseat, killing time
on a long drive. You held me, as you hold me still,
simply going about your business; that fierce, fixed,
dispassionate gaze. Map-reader from a chick.
Path-finder, tracing threads of fluorescence
through the rough grass and the skin of tyres,
crisp packets and signs, unmoved by traffic,
by the updraft and the howl of passing trucks.
Now it's my little two in the backseat asking
if you're somehow stuck. But as we pass and they
shift their sight, back and up, your calculations are
complete. You drop, dead weight, into the soft
estate and the earth receives your energy, repaying
your mastery of movement by placing a vole
exactly where you expect it to be.

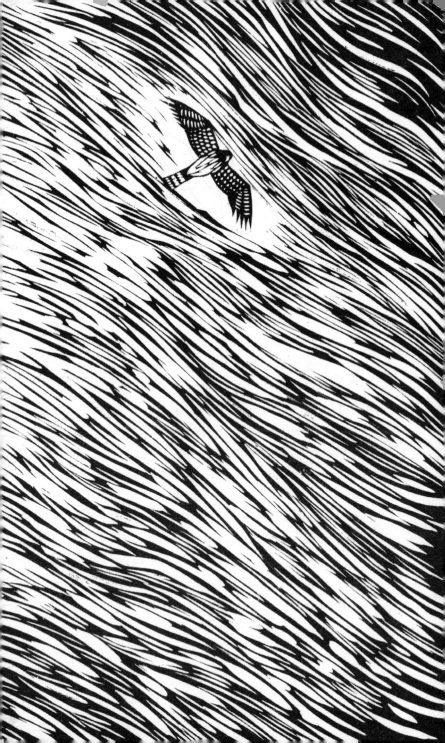

DENNIS

There was a man who skulked our streets,

No job, no car, no hand to hold,

But the same old coat, thick glasses and trait

Of stopping and turning, like he'd just been hailed.

But no one called him.

I mean, why would they?

We didn't even know his name, as I recall.

Or perhaps we did, and forgot,

As we moved on and he did not.

Still, we smirked when we saw him freeze:

That mask of horror; that yawning jaw,

As he thought he caught a voice on the breeze,

Then, broken, plodded on as before.

Children do the cruellest things.

They don't mean any harm, of course,

But they'll point out what adults ignore.

A milling mouth, dirty hair,

Sallow skin stuck with tissue shreds,

Clotting cuts on a rough-shaven chin.

Or when he'd run a wobbling hand under his cap

And start to speak, then crane his neck,

To find nobody there.

Except us kids, grinning back,
Staring at his hopeless stare.

I did an impression of him for a while,
We all did. *Dennis* – that was his name.
Screwing up mouth, aping his style.
Though now it makes me flush with shame.
For I remember a day a woman stopped me dead
And told me of a mangled, metal cave,
Found with his wife's warm body inside
And another, caged, yet too small to save,
Unknown, unborn, already lost
On the M62, in the year's first frost.
And that it was them that he heard
Crying out from desolate moor at dusk.
And tonight, for the first time in years,
I remember him with the hot sting of tears.
In the dark, my arms around my sleeping lad,
I burn with the thought that anybody should know
The agony of losing all they had.

MOOR

You want to show me something,
I assume. Because, on waking,
I find you've filled
the chambers of my heart
with an elemental longing;
that old beckoning, echoing,
like a yow throating: *moor, moor.*

So, I drag them upstream,
through childhood wood,
breaching into blue, metallic air,
heat-clamped grass, reed, ling.
Where curlew mew and the
cauldron stink of green bracken
is pure oxygen.

Then hillcrest.
Earth-mass moored to sky,
iron-cold, rough, quartz-chunk
gritstone. Sucking-mouth bog, wet,
black. Fine, sandy beach-like adder
track, through sharp, dark, bonsai heather.
Here, I have brought my children.

Reenacting my own communion,
they run and trace, with soft finger,
the cup-and-ring markings
of your pagan features.
Old god, awesome god,
they sense your presence
in the wind, the sky, the distance.

You watch me hoist them
to the tops of rocks.
Their small perfection; spread-armed,
laughing, sweat-wet hair,
until my daughter spies you there:
antlered, for a beat, on ridge.
Slipping over horizon.

'*Can we follow?*' She asks.
No, no. Let him go. '*Why?*'
Because I know you, moor.
Why sheep bleat your name
through bleak storm-nights.
I know the way you lure, moor,
the way you turn and trap and bite.

They must know, as I did, an instinct
to stop. Limit. That you are not a
benevolent god. For all the day trippers,
rock chisellers, adding names to the ranks
who've pledged themselves to you:
'E. M. Lancaster 1st XXIV Foot, 1882.'
You cannot be appeased.

Or trusted. Or fully understood. Respected,
perhaps, for what you are: indifferent;
life-giver, life-taker. You who, tenderly
in spring, rears the chicks of the oystercatcher,
gull and plover; you who flecks with purple
flower each stem of heather. You who does
not fail, either, to draw your quota.

Like the friend of mine who
disappeared in your reservoir.
Who climbed your flanks,
filling a bag with stones.
Weighed down, desperate for answers,
he waded into your black waters
knowing you'd show him a door.

Or the countless creatures before. Moor,
us kids who grew up under your shadow
knew both sides of you. We knew
the scenic ecstasies of days like these
– all warm breeze, bilberries. We knew
winter's wire air, snowfalls, ice-gripped grass
frosted fast over frozen becks.

But we knew your changeable heart too,
under the metal bones of industry, scorched
heather, the scattered relics of pleasure.
The part of you that would kill us with
no more fuss than sharpening a new blade of grass.
That legacy, that aura of grace and danger,
looms over all my memories.

Is this what you wanted to show me?
The extent of my possession? I hadn't forgotten.
Or were you calling so I'd bring these children –
that you might shape their budding notions of nature
and wildness as something greater than human
consolation? More like a life-long negotiation
with a primacy beyond comprehension.

THE RIVER

You are outside the swimming pool
in someone's thick, blue jumper,
way too big. Hem halfway
down your jeans. The way you used to
wear mine, as I remember;
hands bunched for warmth in the sleeves.
Your hair swept back into a ponytail.
That cotton-thin scar on your chin.
And your trembling eyes, shocked
at the sight of shock in mine
at seeing *you* here.
You, who's come to me so many times
in sleep, pulled into present; real.
Hurrying up steps in the town where we met,
while behind, two kids doze in the backseat
of your car. The heater on.
The engine running.
The door open.

◎

How tall were you then?
How did we fit when
I put my arms around you?

I forget. How lost were we?
How in love?
For me, entirely.
Or all I believed love to be then,
    in my naivety.
How out of depth I was
trying to coax out those
raw unhealed emotions
and tend to wounds I had no
understanding of.
While you already knew
all the light and shade
of the universe; its poetry.
Before life proper had even
begun for me; before memory
laid down layers of living
so thick that some days I can't see
you at all beyond jumper, scar and
those hidden worlds behind your eyes.
A full-bloom flower meadow
just before the cut.
That was us.
All the sweetness, heat,

briefness,
colours.
The heady hum of high summer
already racing towards its end.

⊙

A half-glance and you go in,
leaving the car and the kids
where you can see them
through the glass entrance
of the reception,
where you've hastened with a question
or to enquire about something forgotten.
I'm due to move on too; to make
a call and walk back to town
across the same river
where we once sat, together,
whispering song lines into each other.
But I stay. A father myself,
I can't resist the urge to watch over
your children. An arm around them
from a distance, until you return.
Which is sooner than I'd wish.
Hurrying past me, arms crossed,
you pause mid-step, stop
and make to turn

like you're thinking
of saying something,
but can't find the words.
Which is the same for me.
There's too little time to open
a dialogue with history.
So we stand together, touching distance
apart, looking down to where the river
still runs. And the ragged skyline
cuts an ordinary day.
Closing the door, pulling away,
your eyes find mine in the mirror.

THE HOTTEST DAY
OF THE YEAR

Velux open, starlings bubbling, sun
and this blistering hot-wood stink
conjure, momentarily, Headingley:
an attic room at the top of a house,
filled with light and possibility,
that day you rushed to be with me,
embarrassed by your own desire,
all the way from Coventry.
Outside now, on an empty road,
the price of growing distance:
they're shutting down a shop.
Papering the windows, its owner,
red-faced with the heat,
lets her mask slip; the strain shows.

A dream dismantled, foreclosed.
She sobs as she posts back the keys.
Passing her on the street, a couple
automatically swerve six feet.
Christ, I long for a future when we
might know what it is to be together
again. To console and to meet;
to recall what it is to crave each other's
touch so much that when it arrives,
carried by train from a different city,
it sears into the mind and memory,
unexpectedly, every component
of a moment and everything it means.

MATTER

There's a realm below the topsoil
Where matted matter matters most.
Beneath the borders of our small-scale toil
Is a graveyard of all things lost.

Uncountable tendrils and tap roots mat,
Resisting trowel, spraining wrist.
Pushing back and confirming that
Things can grow, contest, yet coexist.

Layers of hair-like threads connect
Unpartable clumps, woven together,
Ancient cloth, impermeable to insects
That spill like mercury for leafy cover.

Once I found a perfect ball down there:
Stone, slipped from a pouch of musket shot.
Lost as a soldier hurriedly loaded here,
Pondering, no doubt, his unfortunate lot.

Today the radio's on the sill, by a cup of tea.
Point and counterpoint being loudly made
About the way to remember our dark history
And reconcile the crimes of the human 'trade'.

'How can we come to terms with our past?'
Asks one. *'Well, we can agree, I'm sure,'*
Says another, *'that if life appears hard and fast*
Now, it's nothing compared to what was before.'

True. But he's missed the point and it irks me
As I listen, struggling with these tangled roots:
To reveal that which we don't always see
Is to spend a day in someone else's boots.

And if we only knew as much of the story
Of others as we do of our own;
If we were taught the shame with the glory
We might reconsider what makes our home.

We might too, perhaps, move on from fear,
Anger, suspicion; we may understand
How people might yet feel injustices here
With privilege, power, the possession of land.

But despite this matted matter, I'll still scatter
Seeds in the hope of change and in faith
That new roots may entangle old, and that all
Borders might, one day, blur with growth.

THIS ALLOTMENT

The gate would not open: deadlock.
Key stuck firmly in padlock. And me,
harried, struggling, until I was ready
to abandon the whole damn thing
before it had begun. An intervention:
someone passing with the right tools
said: *'Don't fret. This happens a lot.*
You just need to know the knack.'
Hands twisted with experience,
then, just like that, I was through.
Carrying all I had. Arriving in a
new place. Searching for a plot.

◉

The setting: a patchwork of what was
field tilting down towards beck, rising
again, to Killinghall and moor. As big a
sweep of sky as you can get. Survivor
of time and all weathers; square of
possibility, bequeathed in (good) will,
jealously overlooked by houses, roads,
backyards for being what it is: old soil.
Blessed. Left alone through centuries to

tick over to the rhythm of that old chant:
dig, turn, manure, break, plant,
water, weed, pick, rot. The soil begrudges
not the cast of beetles, worms, spiders,
frogs, slugs, snails. Or ancient ancestries
of rats and wood pigeons; it welcomes back
the time-slip kites, the fox-in-heat nights.
The frenzies of birth and death, the seeds,
yellow teeth and bones of long-ago devoured cows.
What a strange and familiar home this is, split
by its rickety barricades; conjoined by bedroom
    shelves,
seventies bathtubs, reclaimed floors, filing cabinets,
front doors. The make-do-and-mend philosophy
of prehistory. Enough junk to make good fences.
Enough air, space and luminous living things
to feed a family; to spark and fire the senses.

☺

Some days a riot. Some days frozen, eerie quiet.
But a ragged tribe at work, always. A moan, nod
or *'Hello! How's it going? What've you got?*
D'you want to swap?' Or some seeds going spare

that you can't refuse or pay for, or a bumper crop
left anonymously by the compost. Or a hand to lend.
And now and then, a can of beer at very end of day.
Summer sunset; a shared, looking away to the west.
Rooks; swifts scrambling up to sky nests. Today:
a woman repairing a greenhouse, twins in tow,
humouring the old man and his unrequired advice
because she knows he's really aching for a daughter,
gone to live in Australia and there's no one home.
The new widow who gave us raspberry ripple apples
by the bucket that first year, in a headscarf; a lad who
smokes weed in his shed while he makes raised beds
for the ladies opposite, who are always impeccably
dressed and sometimes, subtly, hold hands. And the
couple from Ghana who grow tall, succulent corn
like you've never tasted. All these people rooted
in messy rows of chard and spinach and strawberries
and potatoes. All poised now like me, sweaty and red,
leaning on a spade with dirt smeared across my forehead
watching the sky catching light. Aching, but content.
And not one of us knows the time, or cares.

◉

For eight years a man patiently tilled the plot
next to mine. A grey-haired Mauritian;
a nurse at the hospital who, post-shift,

nursed this earth. A man of luxuriant stories
and recipes. Spice insights: *'You must dry-fry
in batches. Try! Promise me!'* He brought found
things for the children to collect: pennies, bent pins,
a key, buttons and clay pipes. Handfuls of clay pipes.
*'They must have smoked all the time those bloody
    Victorians!'*
Once he disappeared for a while. Months. His absence
registered in the bolted pak choi and unruly weeds.
The ground resented his wayward affection; it threw up
groundsel, dandelion and sow thistle with shocking speed.
I became worried, and aware of how deeply I cared.
Enquiries met shrugs, head shakes. Out of friendship
I appeased the season making a petulant point on his
    patch.
I tidied dwarf beans, watered when needed and almost
wept when I came down one morning and found him
lounging in a chair. *'I've been back home!'* He laughed.
'The sun! The sun there . . .' And so I thought nothing
when it happened again some months later. But then
his cousin, with a plot down the other end of the site,
was there one day wondering if I'd help clear his shed.
'Didn't you hear?' he said, tears rising at my confusion.
'He left us. Three weeks ago. He went in the night.'

◉

When heart-sore, I often wonder if this place is
secretly a model for what should be; how things could be,
were we not so preoccupied with property:
the space to be alone, yet many; to work the small
corners in unity. To be granted parity from the off;
where difference is welcomed for its new thoughts, fruits,
new perspectives, new voices adding new depths to the old
chants. Where the chance to be author of our own fate is
grasped with both hands. Life in *common*, a law beholden
to land, season and locality, governed by the health of the
soil and each another. Oh, there'd be fierce competition
    still,
we're human after all, but where winning might mean
sharing. Earning the right to brag, but where prizes are
bagged and left by the gate with flowers for new arrivals.
We're given such scant measures. So few years in the sun.
Such poor odds. And we're the privileged ones, arriving
without the press of brutality or cruel legacy, or ground
ravaged by drought and war. Even then, life is fragile and
gossamer-thin. No sooner are we through the
    gate, narrowing
our eyes into wind, than we're mediating: *Let THIS seed
    grow,*
please, not these weeds. Spare us from frost and disease.
'Word to the wise,' a man once told me, handing over beans,
'Plant three: one for the birds, one for the earth, one for thee.

Then get on tha' knees and attend to what comes up tirelessly.'
Maybe that's the truce we need to reach. Or the harmony.

◉

For one evening, too soon, the gate will be open.
We'll notice day has darkened, the sunset gone
behind the hill. And just as we're wondering,
who's that been left for? A voice on the wind
will start to whisper: *Come on, now. Come on.*
Someone else's turn. We'll hear the old chant:
dig, turn, manure, break, plant, water, weed,
pick, rot . . . and realise the flowers have been
left not for those arriving, but those leaving.
And we'll wish we had one more season to
witness perfection, but somewhere a bell will
be ringing and we'll already be walking home.

SELF-ISOLATING

'I was thinking,' you say,
'when all this is over
we should get away for a few days.
Far off. North. Where hills are
frozen with the kind of frost
you don't find in towns
anymore. Away from this
heatstroke weather, to hard
hoar-crusted summits
and meadows with glinting sprays

of reeds, where mist steams off olive-green
lakes. To small woods chanced upon
in the pleats of fells. Let's wake
in a tent rimed with ice
on the third morning, alone,
returning to our senses warming
soup on last night's fire,
breath and woodsmoke
mingling in the trees.
Let's hurry back tired
and longing for this bed,
the warmth of these
four walls, the shape of these
rooms. Not craving their escape.'

THE HEEDING

When they came to us in the yarden
the sky was afire. Billowing, pink pollen-air;
a final call from hearts of flowers.
Not quite evening, but getting there.
A tortoiseshell lurched over the creeper,
tumbling in. A ripped corner of coloured paper,
amber one side; black the other.
Then two more. Then a small white
materialised over us like a flake of paint
falling from the wall, catching light.
I counted three bumblebees, but knew others to be
lumbering among the loosestrife and meadowsweet's
greenery. I didn't move, neither head nor eye,
as a peacock butterfly flitted through the space
and yet more flew in (day moths, hoverflies) in case
their seeing us seeing them would break the spell.
We'd been rooted all day. Nowhere to go.
Ideas exhausted. School books spreadeagled.
Pencils scattered. My good intentions had faded
and we'd resorted to planting sticks,
flagging the soil where the ants paraded,
finding the gaps, the cracks. Practising tricks
of focusing, listening, noticing what's really there.

And although I'd believed I'd failed,
that we'd achieved nothing much of worth,
this heeding had been transforming us, dissolving us.
We'd become invisible, indivisible, from earth,
leaf, stone and stamen, petal, wood and wing
in the sensory machinery of these creatures' workings.
Reduced to atoms. Indistinct. Existing in the margins.
Alive to being blessed
by the presence of glorious things.
More came. A handspan from my face a marmalade
hoverfly hung on a continuous hum. And you, only five,
normally so restless, somehow sensed not to stir
the air, not to blink away the tear in the eye that blurs
the world, for a moment, into something strange and magic.
You sat transfixed, like me, by its drone. A one-note
    incantation
vibrating on a deep-time frequency; a bell struck hard
and ringing, shaking loose all fixity. An act of concentrating
that ushered in a new realm of foreshortenings and
    openings,
where the pollen dust and blurry dots of insect wings
    glittering
silver around us were at once as minuscule as particles

and as colossal as new stars birthing. Time was nothing.
I blinked first. The scale was dizzying. I'd felt myself
    falling
into interstices from where there is no returning. The
    hoverfly
was lifting, shifting sideways and then everything was up
and leaving. And we returned to ourselves awoken;
    arisen.

BLACK ANT

It was trapped.
A black ant; its back flattened by the edge
of a shifted pot. Stuck to stone wall,
waving helplessly in useless motion,
repeatedly dragging its injured half
nowhere. Until I found I could
concentrate on nothing
but the weight of that pressing pot,
the insistence of the ant's dying petition.
So I put down what I was doing
and moved its burden. And then,
(committed now) in some act of small apology,
with a little, dry twig I tried lifting the ant free.
Horror. It broke in two. Its still-twitching half
curled around the stick like a life raft.
Its antennae flicked: *What now? What now?*
But I didn't have a clue what to do,
and could only think to put it back, head and stick,
where it was. Laying it together.
Reordering the tiny body, carefully.
The way you do with the dead.
And wondering why I'd interfered
in the first place. Other ants passed.

In a black rivulet. None seemed to notice.
A week later, they encroached the house.
I found one investigating the dark under-cooker,
And I destroyed the nest.

FAMILY TREES

At midnight, while shifting in its sleep,
The sky shrugged off a cloak of heat,
Releasing its long-held breath. A breeze
Blew in, briefly, from the north.
It shivered the clematis hanging over us,
Carrying the day's long inhale of scents
Of beech and oak and ash and pine
Into our little, tree-less yard, and sent
Our wine-drunk minds imagining
We were not there at all, but in a forest.
Amid that self-same perfume smell
Of sun-warmed trunk and split, cracked
Log. Resinous, overgrown with moss.

We closed our eyes: '*Where are you now?*
First answer. Don't think about it!'
You said Ashdown; me, Hagg Wood.
You said you missed your sisters most and
Home. I found myself in overgrown avenues
Of larch-dark, remembering the place where
As a boy I was lost and my father's voice
Retrieved me. Where he'd bundled me
Up in his arms and carried me back.

And I'd seen him so cross, so happy.
We drank to those woods
As we drank in that air before
The breeze breathed off elsewhere.
And, exhausted, we rose and stumbled
To bed to read, again, the news.
And in our sleep we grieved for all
The family trees losing their leaves.
And around those bare roots of memory
We laid our little home-made wreaths.

THE SPARROWS

The way their heads mechanically
twist and tip and little wings twitch
in short, sharp, flicks, they appear
more automaton birds than birds.
A line of clockwork, tin-plate,
junk shop things. Dusty, backroom
fifties novelties discovered by chance
in a box on a shelf, brought down and
arranged on the wall outside; that,
against the odds, were found to work
when wound a rusty half-turn. Now,
keyed back to life, they jolt and jerk
in August sun, repeating that familiar
squeak of something just needing
a little love and a drop of oil
after too long forgotten:
cheep, cheep, cheep.

VIKING GOLD

She'd won a competition. You told us en route.
A small haul of Viking gold.
Replica funerary jewellery, unearthed
via coupons cut from the backs of magazines.
Precious though; hallmarked. Something
to behold and warranting a drive
that Sunday all the way from Ilkley.
The thought of it didn't fit: bright, extravagant.
But she'd worn it when we
arrived for a roast and a look-see.
It adorned the forties dress and pinny
her generation lived in. That prim utility:
a plain blue-red print from shoulder to shin.
A thin faded leather belt looped in.

She was always sternest with me, the youngest,
as she had been with you, the eldest.
The sombre November to Grandad's June,
disapproving of our conspired silliness,
wrestling with the programming
she couldn't get over;
yielding to the mindset of county border
Methodism and the Ingham blood of Brierfield.

Born of bleak moor and indoctrinated patriarchy;
the dark, meagre modesties of mill town terraces.
Be grateful for the least. Repent, repress
the sin of boastful joy; let your worries be endless
lest God give you, with a clout,
something proper to worry about.

A fear justified when the war that Grandad endured
fireballed the young men in Spitfires she raised money
for at town rallies: Keighley, Nelson, Skipton, Colne.
See? Keeping her the scolded girl in a family chapel
forever. Life squeezed out; burnt of its flavour.
Except for that Sunday, when she came to the door
with a crack still at her mouth's corners; a smile only
   I saw.
First to ring the bell, I'd watched her through
the frosted glass as she'd paused in the hallway mirror
at the sight of herself bedecked in that Norse treasure,
before an order barked from her brain corrected
her demeanour back to what was expected.
That ice you could never thaw, and so resented.

There was another time, much later. A September.
Grandad dead. I could drive. She'd wanted me,
you said, to stop by her little canal-side flat.

Remember? Just before her mind unspooled
towards infancy. I rang the bell and waited,
unsure, but when she opened the door I saw
she was wearing her Viking gold again.
And she'd cooked fish pie especially. Luxury.
Eating by the window we laughed at ducks
childishly. And I've wondered since if she was
showing me someone she'd longed to be.
And, perhaps sensing an end to the journey,
she'd taken down that grave-good jewellery,
dressed up a little girl lost and left her in my memory.

DAILY BRIEFING

'We must be humble in the face of nature.'
Such a rich line. I doubt it's yours.
For you've shown little of this before,
Humility or awareness.
And as you wander from briefing room
To back kitchen, to new baby's bedroom,
I scan the moor from the allotment.
Where a withering easterly is stamping
Over the hills. My hands are split
From the cold mud and hours uprooting
Stubborn dandelions, bindweed, couch.
The sheep will be seeking sheltered corners,
The fox hunkering down in its den.
And if it's alright with you,
I'll stay here a little while yet.
For it won't be long before sunset.

MIST

This mist has smothered us for three days now.
As if in a light bulb; six-foot sight. Swamp air,
Bone-cold. Like a dank flannel from the fridge
Wrapped around the skin to quell a bruise.
Before sleep I took a last look at its stubborn density,
Illuminated by a streetlight, a swollen golden orb
Bloated shapeless by fog. And a half-car
Dissolving beneath, blurring into too-wet watercolour.
It hadn't moved an inch this morning. Curtains parted,
Brewing coffee, I saw the yard had vanished.

I was a widower, hollowed out, staring through
Frosted glass at a life I could no longer remember.
Somehow a starling pushed through,
Dragging itself out of a fold in the cloaking
Wet. Ravished. Fluff-feathered. A beggar
Blot, black; a survivor from a shipwreck
Roused awake by the roll of the tide,
Staggering through a shoreline sea fret,
Limping toward the sole light prevailing.
The holy glow of this window.

WOLF

Wolf stalks these
Brittle, blurred days.
Haws, dripping hips, shadow trees,
Enveloped in greys.
It tracks through slime-mud,
Ankle-deep, between winter beet.
Nosing where we stood,
Laughing, to wipe our children's feet.
Pause too long
And it's there.
Wolf-reek sudden, strong
On altering air.
Concealed in copse,
Eyes hot as furnace doors,
Drawing closer along the tops,
Hurrying on tireless paws;
Watching.
Driven by un-killable ire.
Waiting
For the weak-self to tire.
So take them now; run ahead,
Safe in numbers; safe from whatever
Keeps wolf hungry for this head,
Feasting on this heart forever.

PHARMACY CAKE

Small, hunched, frail.
Little more than bones
under mac, hat and brolly.
Unsurely footed, as if balancing
on stilts, I've seen her here before.
Always ten minutes early.
Always first in the queue,
waving at them as they're setting up:
'How are you, dear? How are you?'
Although they can't hear her
between the mask
and reinforced glass,
she speaks to them as children,
her voice louder as one walks past,
arms full of pain relief and sugar-free sweets:
'Is that a new shirt? It's nice.'
Her thick glasses blotted with rain
turning to sleet, bathed in the yellow
strip-lit warmth of the window,
she waits.
Counting seconds.

You'd think seconds would count
at such a stage, at her age. Certainly,
you'd think there'd be more
pressing things to do ten days before
Christmas than to be here, too early,
in this weather. But when the lock
is turned and she, ill-suited to the role,
pushes at the heavy, thief-proof frame,
there is a small squeal of joy. And
when it's opened from the other side,
she says: *'I'm here! I'm here!'*
Stuck behind, the queue bemoans
the unfolding rigmarole of folding all
(hat, mac, brolly) into a wheeled holdall;
this performance of taming
white hairs, flattening flyaways
to the solemn shape of her skull;
her slow, insect approach of the till.
And declaration: nothing to pick up, nor buy.
The queue fidgets, groans, sighs.
'No. I'm just dropping off today.'

A woman appears from the back.
'*Is it my favourite?*'
'*Oh, Jackie! You're here!*'
And it's revealed: the home-made cake,
looking too small, too heavy, to be right,
poorly wrapped in foil and towel.
Lifted trophy-like from her holdall.
'*Thought I better bring you this . . .*'
Now the queue goes deathly quiet,
understanding this fuss, this pilgrimage;
this braving of sleet and virus;
this coddling of staff, is a way to treat a pain
more mangling, more unbelievably sore
than any of us are collecting prescriptions for.
But that's not what unpicks me.
It's what I hear when even she
feels the pressure and weight of
the waiting queue to be too great,
and makes out she's something else to do:
'*Right then. I'd better go . . .*'
Then, quietly at the door to no one: '*I love you.*'

THE PROBLEM WITH US

Scant pickings this afternoon. Nothing but rot
and bones in this endless mockery of a year.

And the knowledge that a human being somewhere
is sitting down to write stories about how vaccines

sicken and deform, knowing them to be untrue.
Changing words, mutating facts and meanings,

inventing figures and quotes. Shock-tactic simplicity.
Uploading multiple conspiracies, intending to confuse,

to undermine and reduce efficacy. The objective being
to seed doubt in people half a world away. To destabilise

and sentence to death. To win a hand in the old game of
politicking. And today, at the garage, I saw the way it
    spreads

as a man spat out in rage: *'They're all in it together. I'll never
get one. Things I've read! Give me your email and I'll send it
    on.'*

What chance do we have? What right to call anything
    'insidious'
when such malignancies seem a habit of our species?

When the same human being who writes such lies can
    rise, weary
from a day's murder, go downstairs and cook dinner for
    their children?

THE IVY

The world is encased in liquid glass,
wet, not furred with frost, for rain
besieges us again this morning.
Hard rain. How dreary this feels;
how at a standstill. Christmas cancelled.
And it being a Monday too. *Oh*,
the road sighs, *oh*, as drops dot
and shiver and streak the windows.
The kids want nothing of the flooded
land outside, but when you return
from the river, afloat and glowing
with inner warmth, I layer up.
For this is how it is:
I seek the wood
as you seek the water.

But it lies closer, over a wall, thickly.
Down a snicket through the estate
(quiet, decorations lit)
is a glossy coat of ivy. Plump, green,
immune to whatever's killed
the hedge of withered beech,
these stems of rotting hogweed.
Look at me, it says. *Give me your focus.*
And I do: its full, heart-shaped leaves,
luscious in siling rain as spring cabbages;
black berries globed in tight clusters
ready to feed, all winter, the blackbirds
pigeons and thrushes. *Remember,*
it says, *fidelis*. Even in darkening days
life triumphs, always.

SNOW CHARM

Snow

loosening, collapsing from branches,
slipping, dripping from the shock-shushed trees.
Blowing like dust off feathery canopies.

Snow

in deep drifts, thick-blanketing,
cushioning the uneven wreckage
of the fell wood's floor: stump, hump, thorn.

Snow

making chandeliers of crowns,
melting, *tic-tac*, *tic-tac*, over the wild track
of a swollen beck. And us, tired from the climb.

Snow

blind, breathing hard, pausing
to shed a layer. Coming to, like you do after
deep sleep. From numbness to clarity.

Snow

over the drystone walls beyond,
over the heather, over scattered dwarf spruce;
the summit dome of powdered white

Snow

shine, too bright to look at.
The children hurrying up the wet track,
squeaking, roaring; stopping to pack

Snow

balls to throw back at us. All thoughts but
being here, now, on these high, dry-cold tops,
snagged on the wire of the last fence below.

Snow

trees on the fellside; dark pine,
drifting with wraith mist, like steam rising off the
hot black flank of a run horse. Each bough

Snow

dressed, sparkling with the last of the sun.
And I know we must go, I only wish some part of us
could remain, out of harm's way, frozen in this

Snow

as we two age and you two grow; let us stay
like spirits fast-bound to a conjuring stone,
leaving and returning each year, unchanged as

Snow

THE END OF THIS
(DRINKING POEM)

Now pass me a glass and let me
drink to the end of this.
[Cheers]
I mean hard-drink, Norse-drunk.
Edge-of-madness intoxication
to cure edge-of-sadness exhaustion.
[Cheers]
Let me purge. Let me shake off
this year the way the otter
slips out of fast, rising water
and makes the holt just in time,
then wakes to find the flood has passed.
[Cheers]
Let me rid my days of caution and fear,
these protocols and tiers
and Zoom funerals for people I love
and will never see again.
[Cheers]
These cancelled birthdays.
These bans on being together.
These redundancies, uncertainties,

limits on impulse and joy,

on movement and autonomy.

[Cheers]

This enforced house arrest,

these same four walls,

this loneliness, like an open wound.

The disordered mess of this country,

the unfairness of its bureaucracy,

the sorrow, stress and anxiety.

The make-no-sense policies

and track-and-trace catastrophes.

[Cheers]

Let's drink to the end of all of this.

[Cheers]

And what then? What will follow?

Well, let a giddy mind paint tomorrow

in full begin-again colour. A new picture.

Pass me a glass. Give me courage

to start over. And be better.

[Cheers]

LIGHT

You'll not take the light
from me. Not now.
Now that I've
got my eye in.
Now I can see it
everywhere.
This evening,
Sorrento light

backdrops the gaps
between the terraces and
the back-to-backs. Great,
Mediterranean sea-horizons.
The peach heat;
a smooth curtain
of metal sheet
glowing bronze.

Yesterday I saw the dawn:
dark dissolving into day.
The new blood
saturation of the
massed capillaries

that are budding trees
caught in the folds of fields,
as rooks slipped free from an oak

like souls. And tomorrow
I will be attendant
to the fact that
the sun is higher
than it's been
for as long as anyone
can remember.
There will be laughter

in the dark corners
again. And hope.
No, you'll not take the light
from me. Not now.
Now that I've
got my eye in.
Now I can see it
everywhere.

DUEL PART II

Another kiss of death.
In echo of the first, I witness:
smack – the aftermath of talons
hard-hitting a frail cage of yellow-blue
feathers. Splitting trees
with a sudden saw-scream of panic.

The butter-brown blur of a hawk
(grasping, this time a crushed blue tit,
one ridiculous wing still flapping)
plunges through the canopy.
Down, down, into a beech leaf sea
thirty foot above me.

Such repetition. The universe's
incessant teaching.
Even now, in this half-hour of
lunchtime running when,
desk-folded, creaking, I was only seeking
the calm and stillness of the wood.

Even now it follows me.
I wonder, why?

What did I miss?
What did I not see?
What did I not learn?
Impart? Understand?

Death. Death. The unfairness
of inevitable death. Is that it?
Questions sparked at speed
as spring looks on. Nuthatch, shrew,
a nest of young. Everything heeds
this duel. Stupefied, the wood is trembling

under the heart-thump arrowing
of the hawk's intrusion, writhing,
stubbornly gripping
its screeching, screaming prey.
Down, down, into the depths,
like a gannet gorging, sinking

towards me, until its momentous energy
brings it too close and, instinctively,
the hawk lets go.
Beak up, beating wings,
it floats back through the beech breakers,
vanishing through the swirling surface.

In the same movement,
the blue tit, discarded and ragged,
pitches into a holly beside me
like a cannonball. Too weary to reach its nest,
aghast at oblivion's nearness, breast hammering,
it sits for ten minutes fearless

of me parting the prickled leaves to see.
Then, unflexing the wounded wing,
it folds it, neatly, back into place.
A shake; a single note
as its brain fizzes back from blank
to find itself, miraculously, free.

The lesson then? If there is one
imprinted this time, it's different:
nature's god-like violence spares
as well as takes. There is release.
Death? Inevitable, yes, but not yet.
Or not today, at least.

Our love and thanks to our friends and our families, to our brilliant agent, Jessica Woollard, and all at David Higham Associates. Likewise, to those early readers (you know who you are); we're hugely grateful for your words of encouragement. This book would not have happened without the understanding, support and vision of Sarah Rigby and the team at Elliott & Thompson, especially Pippa Crane, Marianne Thorndahl, Ella Chapman, Alison Menzies and Lorne Forsyth. Our thanks to all at Simon & Schuster too. Lastly, we want to acknowledge the support of booksellers who've struggled through the most difficult of years, yet who've embraced this book – and many others – with love, energy and passion, and who remain committed to that vital work: bringing words and minds together.

First published 2021 by
Elliott and Thompson Limited
2 John Street
London WC1N 2ES
www.eandtbooks.com

This paperback edition published in 2022

ISBN: 978-1-78396-633-2

Text © Rob Cowen 2021
Illustrations © Nick Hayes 2021

9 8 7 6 5 4 3 2 1

A catalogue record for this book is available from the British Library.

Typesetting by Carr Design Studio

Printed in the UK by CPI Group (UK) Ltd, Croydon, CR0 4YY